MODUS TOLLENS

IPDs: Improvised Poetic Devices

Yuriy Tarnawsky

Modus Tollens

IPDs: Improvised Poetic Devices

Yuriy Tarnawsky

$$p \dashrightarrow q$$
$$\sim q / \sim p$$

Jaded Ibis Press
sustainable literature by digital means™
an imprint of Jaded Ibis Productions

ISBN: 978-1-937543-45-7

Library of Congress Control Number: 2013911193

Published by Jaded Ibis Press, *sustainable literature by digital means*™
An imprint of Jaded Ibis Productions, LLC, Seattle, WA USA

Cover and interior photography by Karina Tarnawsky. Book design by Debra Di Blasi.

This book is available in multiple editions and formats. Visit our website for more information: jadedibisproductions.com

MODUS TOLLENS

who else but for k?
wish they were happier
but you give what you've got

CONTENTS

PREFACE: heuristic poetry and modus tollens   9
water   11
window   14
evening sky   16
monday mourning   18
landscape with a man   19
landscape with a dead man   21
woman dreaming in her sleep   25
bulging eye   28
flower1   31
flower2   33
flower3   35
window into night   37
clock   39
watermelon   41
if it is night   43
erection precedes   46
arse poetica   50
angels   53
leipzig july 28   57
on kicking the bucket   62
on kicking the bucker once more   67
on kicking the bucket in a different way   70
brokenhaiku1   73
brokenhaiku2   74
brokenhaiku3   75
supreme gardener   76
mountain   78
cloud   79
raindrop   80
water   81
fish   82
bird   84

stone	85
flower	86
grass	87
old cemetery	88
your dead	89
rose1	91
rose2	92
rose3	93
sillysong1	94
sillysong2	95
sillysong3	96
dreamdream1	97
dreamdream2	103
dreamdream3	109
tiger1	114
tiger2	115
tiger3	116
cityscape1	117
cityscape2	119
cityscape3	120
seascape1	121
seascape2	122
seascape3	123
dawn	124
sunsets	125
dusk	126
god is	127
the world is not	128
chores	130
blackblacknight1	131
blackblacknight2	132
blackblacknight3	133
death/blue car	136
die young	139
little fugue	147

PREFACE
heuristic poetry and modus tollens

I call these poems Improvised Poetic Devices on analogy with Improvised Explosive Devices because, similarly to the way the latter shatter and shred hard matter, they wreak havoc in the reader's mind through the confusingly arranged and chopped-up language of which they are composed. This state is only temporary, however, and as he progresses through the poem considering the many possibilities of interpretation that present themselves to him, the reader will reject most of them, selecting only the most likely ones, eventually eliminating all but one, which will be the poem he has built up for himself and which in most cases will be the one I had in mind. Thus, through the process of reading, the reader will become my coauthor of the poem.

The language in these poems is (mis)arranged and chopped up in a careful manner so as to send the reader's mind in different poetically productive directions, which will add to the scope and overall evocative effect of the poems somewhat in the way this is achieved in *Finnegan's Wake* through Joyce's misspelled and pun-laden language.

This kind of poetry may be described as Heuristic because, for it to exist, it must be searched for and ultimately found by the reader; it is the product of the reader's toil.

In contrast with its Projective counterpart, Heuristic Poetry is designed primarily for visual perception. When read aloud, it should be accompanied by visual aids (hard copy or projected text) for optimal effect.

Modus tollens (Latin: "mode of taking away/denying") is a term from propositional logic, referring to a rule of deductive reasoning with negation introduced into it. Its equivalent without negation is called *modus ponens* (Latin: "mode of putting down/affirming"). It is a valid form of reasoning and consists of two premises—a conditional "if-then" statement wherein p implies q, and the premise that q is false. From these it may be concluded that p is false.

The classical example of modus tollens is, "If it is night, Apollo sleeps. Apollo doesn't sleep. Therefore it is not night." The reader will find my treatment of it in this book. (In it "iff" stands for "if and only if.") It is for the reader to find out what is the relationship between the book's title and its content.

Yuriy Tarnawsky
White Plains, NY
April 2, 2013

water

water drip
ping from a kitchen
faucet broken? not closed
tightly? over a pile of
dirty dishes plates in
the sink stacked like my
many faces tears? whose
tears? no one there but
a black hole in a chrome
plated steel pipe outside rain
drops falling off bare black
branches the sky over
my face hands tears? whose
tears? cold dead branch
es white void there nothing
more no water drip
ping over my broke
n childhood a 1930's car rusty
tires wheels gone windows wind
shield gone body rusty red
dented sunken to the floor
board behind the house out
house half eaten up from
below by luxuriant grass
weeds stinging ukrainian nettles my
mother's death like the

broken rusty engine in the engine
well no hood her stomach
rusty no just red with pain torn
open no hood broken no
roar from it the greek
tragic mouth my father's
death no flags bending
down like horses their long
maned necks in
sorrow no horses bending down
their long maned
necks in sorrow just one flag
grazing on the bare hard funeral
parlor floor like a horse bend
ing its long maned
neck in hunger crocuses blue
yellow like his fingers pushing their
way out of the still frozen march
ground to watch him sail no sail away in
the tight black boat of the coffin his
fingers like blue yellow crocuses
pushing their way back into the still
frozen march soil bored with
watching him drift away in
the tight black boat of the
coffin water not tears
dripping over my face bare
black hands my

feet devouring the bare hard
road in a bulimia of aim
lessness

window

this poem jagged composed
in gothic mental
script lines like
glass in a brok
en window frightening shar
p shards sticking out
of the frame you can cut your
wrists on it imagine slash impale
your throat imagine pierc
e your jugular vein tryin
g to get out of your
self it the
hell out of it through
it into the
world wintry garden rocks
bushes trees thick soft white
snow like letters spell
ing out unknown words rock
bush tree snow god
knows what
they mean mean
nothing? just outside the
window you can
reach them with your
hand pet caress
them like pets they

purrrrrr and god
knows what they
mean? mean
nothing? nothing? enough 2:
18 time to get
busy fix my late
lunch supper for who
ever may come back
home will return turn
ashes to
ashes dust
to dust they to
me me to
them we to
supper then to
bed the lights
out nothing

evening sky

the evening sky full of great
black sharks jaws wide
open aimed at teeth
reaching for the rest of
the light disappear
ing behind the horiz
on layers of cold oxy
gen nitrogen all
around of hard quartz
salt nacl h2
o frozen down
below time for daughter
s to plot against
their fathers with their
mothers tell funny
stories about
them laugh point them
out to friends
enemies out of dark
corners for wives
to fill out papers for
putting their husbands in in
sane asylums brew deadly
potion fill cups with
dust for them to choke on in
their sleep cold cold wind

wind blowing from all
directions at once the sound
of windows doors on
crosses opening and
closing closing with a
bang christ sticky
blood dripping from the sparse
blond beard getting
ready for his guests
fixing strong flexible
canes tight crowns of
thorns huge black
nails sponges soaked in
vinegar on the ends of long
spear
s

monday mourning

after a sundae sun
day a sleep
less night toss
ing from sartre
kierkegard freud
a split
ting head
ache till a wan mon
day dawn made
it a pilgrim
age to the
beach there
the sea was throw
ing up all over af
ter a night of bing
ing on iodine
whiskey salt
herring sea
weed jelly
fish paper plastic
bottles bags con
doms a whole lot of
sand

landscape with a man

back turned to the
world himself on
the edge of spa
ce no
thing ground to
the right left be
hind white wi
th giant ug
ly garbage dai
sies an out
house lat
rine on his
right door o
pen hang
ing on on
e hinge right
side lower like
his left
shoulder a mirror
image of
him a
double teeth bit
ten hard to
gether face flush
ed red eyes bulg
ing he hu

rls oranges at the hu
ge orange
disk of
the sun be
fore him
one two on and
on and
on

they go swoo
sh like rock
ets spla
ttt leave run
nnny dark
spots on the
glori
ous bright sur
face

out of a hat
red he can
't explain ju
st feel
s

landscape with a dead man

the
re are fr
esh ear
ly spr
ing mor
nigs w
hen you'r
e ten twel
ve thir
teen an
d they wak
e you u
p to go s
ee life the tru
th the land cl
ear of build
ings cover
ed with grave
l sand cla
y made fl
at in all
directions all
the way to the horiz
on for you to bet
ter under
stand see
him he in the cen

ter in a br
own suit ly
ing face
down the left
arm str
etched out for
ward reach
ing for the horiz
on fu
ture bet
ter tim
es bet
ter than n
ow the righ
t one gon
e hid
den hid
ing under
him sca
red the left
leg bent rais
ed ready to
move for
ward too
late should
have moved th
en the right
one str

aight toe
s point
ing back reach
ing for th
e horiz
on past bet
ter time
s bet
ter than n
ow righ
t cheek press
ed to the gr
ound dear mom
mmy mm
m your littl
e boy prod
igal son has
come back
home home af
ter all th
ese yea
rs back o
f the head blow
n out g
one one
big hole
thick long
brown ha

ir a
shamed tr
ying to hid
e it in vain not
thick long br
own e
nough bra
ins spill
ed ou
t on the gr
ound lik
e crag
gy mount
ain peak
s ros
y in the ro
sy ri
sing sun

woman dreaming in her sleep

super horizon
tal flat the
white hospital be
d her bod
y sunken dow
n to nea
rly merg
ed wi
th the fl
at white tile
d floor a mer
e near shad
ow on it all un
covered the
sheet scrunch
ed up by her
feet on her
back right
arm raised a
bove her hea
d rest
ing on the man
gled pil
low left curl
ed up by hudd
ling a

gainst her left
side both
legs turned
right knees
pressed to
gether feet
apart though the
sheer white night
gown push
ed way up a
bove her
waist the sh
y black tri
angle hi
ding not suc
ceding out of the
left top cor
ner of her sku
ll spread
s an opal opal
escent puddle a gi
ant amoe
ba her dr
eam a field of
milk mist
ty autum or
chard giant lumi
nous blue e

ye gal
lons of s
perm spill
ed on the g
round part of a
canvas by fran
cis bac
on

bulging eye

hug
e the siz
e of half o
f t
he earth's g
lobe push
ing it
s way out f
rom und
er the bon
e ski
n strain
ing trembl
ing whit
e all a
round fright
ening des
pair gath
ered col
lected in a d
ark circ
le in the mid
dle on t
op bl
ack in t
he cen

ter peak

ing reach

ing ou

t for what

's a

bove wh

at's not a

man

's? being tor

tured? leg

s arms t

wisted ou

t of the sock

ets? hor

se's? brok

e its leg? will b

e dest

royed? picador

's horse's? go

t gored? its gu

ts spil

ling out? a

bull's? bei

ng skin

ned alive? for

bidden to bel

low? or

all of human

ity's? anim
al king
dom's? liv
ing creat
ures? th
is poe no path
etic hand
ful of wor
ds try
ing to f
orm them
selves in
to a mean
ing?

flower1

all
gray as in
a black a
nd white photo
graph a wo
man middle
aged? young? hair
wind
blown face wind
blown too hag
gard clothes hagg
ard too right
arm stretch
ed out to the
side hand hold
ing a flo
wer big black
eyed susan? sm
all sun
flower? wilt
ed life
less like a hang
ed man hel
d up her face
turned a
way left lip

s scrunched
down bitten tear
s unab
le to burs
t out o
f the craze
d eye
s

flower2

a plowed f
ield slop
ing up a
steep h
ill a tele
phone pole up
close on the
left thick
tall you can't
see its bot
tom top
a man walk
ing a
way from
it in a
long stride bend
ing for
ward arms
swing
ing the jack
et of the bag
gy suit op
en flap
s flap
ping up a
head on

the crest a
nother pole th
in shar
p tear
ing the gr
ay sky no
thing in
side

flower3

a dog run
ning a
cross an em
ty city squ
are tall skin
ny ribs stick
ing out all sk
in and
bones hair
wet drip
ping from no
where to now
here unaw
are of it
self the
world just run
ning from her
e to the
re cut
ting a
cross a flat sur
face pla
ne a liv
ing skin
and bone
s dot

ted line geo
metric physic
s con
cept bisectri
x

a text
book of meta
physics smell
ing like a w
et dog

window into night

white ti
led walls bri
ght neo
n light on the
ceiling every
thing pain
fully clea
r sharp gas
range sink fau
cet drip
ping wat
er small fri
ghtened fr
idge hi
ding in th
e corne
r in the
middle of th
e floor a p
lain wood
en table no
thing on
top of
no chair next
to it the squa
re wind

ow beautiful
ly wide o
pen to let
in the black star
less night

clock

a kit
chen white
tiled walls
bright ne
on ceiling li
ght sink fau
cet drip
ping wa
ter small fright
ened frid
ge plain wood
en table in
the midd
le of the fl
oor an old
fashioned cloc
k on
it round
three leg
ged bell on
top black ro
man numeral
s on a white
face hand
s dead st
ill nine for

ty seven se
conds lik
e seeds in
side a water
melon the squa
re wind
ow beautiful
ly wide o
pen to let
in the black star
less night

watermelon

a round stripe
d green and
white water
melon on top
of a plain wood
en table in th
e middle of the floo
r red fi
re black cin
ders of a mexi
can vulcan
o inside a trian
gular black hand
led knife be
side it every
thing pain
fully shar
p in the gla
re of the ne
on light on
the cei
ling whi
te tiled walls ran
ge sink fau
cet small fright
ened frid

ge in the
corner the squa
re wind
ow beautiful
ly wide o
pen to let
in the black star
less night

if it is night

iff
it is night apollo
sleeps lit
tle boy's cur
ly golden hair
ed head sunk
en deep in
to the soft
white pil
low dreams pass
ing through mind
brain like
clouds pas
t the moon stars
body limp soft mer
ged with part of
the soft white
linen mother le
to father zeu
s watch
ing over under all a
round him ap
ollo isn't sleep
ing a grown
man head
hot mind

full of hard
thoughts knot
s body ten
se merged wi
th part of the
hard bunk b
ed no mo
ther father life'
s disturb
ing an
swers itt iss nott
nightt blind
ing white day sun
light empti
ness all a
round him her
us stretch
ing in all direct
ions be
hind the lone
ly shin
y aluminum din
er space for a hun
dred thousand gal
lon vat full
of ketchup to be
spilled over un
der all a

round the pris
tine white
snow

erection precedes

empty earl
y sun
day mourn
ing walk
ing emp
ty dirty side
walks street
s like once long
long time a
go the emp
ty room
s shiny floor
boards in my bach
elor pough
keepsie pad th
oughts a
bout the two car
ved figu
rines a co
zy dark cat
hedral of th
e cathedral
less black
coffe in
stead of whi
te host be

ing and no
thing in
stead of the good
old book no no
t carved figu
rines two mag
gots re
volting re
nowned not obs
cure dios
curi bob
sy twins cas
tor beav
er and pol
lux poul
ou existence pre
cedes erection e
rection pre
cedes bad
faith worse philo
sophy he shove
s his itsy
bitsy teeny wien
ie into her beav
er bet
ween the t
wo gray pink
cheeks hemi

spheres screw
ed screwed
up loboto
mized she le
ads scar
ed willing teen
aged girls be
hind his books st
ood up screen
like for him to
feast on their flat
chests tight
fist sex the trem
bling drugad
dict's hand of
the chica
go dawn rea
ches out thr
ough the dirt
y window
pane for her
hair sp
illed like cof
fee on the grea
sy pillow her
head dream
ing hot dream
s of good old
fashioned sex

love marri
age next to big
nelson's cool
cold dist
ant one erection pre
cedes inva
gination existence pre
cedes death all a
lone now no
thing before be
hind me once
there was a
time when books
fell on their
soft kn
ees to pray
to

arse poetica

big fat whi
te ass of
the sky stick
ing out o
ver the hori
zon strain
ing all crap
below all
crap? all
crap turds tin
y purple one
s violets big
white yellow
ones lil
ies red frag
rant roses girls
named rosie wi
th daisies in
stead of eye
s old
men named jo
hn joe geo
rge sprawl
ed drunk on the side
walk mouth
s wide o

pen drool
ing eyes see
ing the gray con
crete of li
fe ten
year old boys
alone in empty
rooms home
from their
mothers' fune
rals not
knowing yet how to
cr
y hair
on their heads stir
ring try
ing to stand
up black
thoughts climb
ing walls in em
pty bl
ack pri
son cells mind
s p
ain wail
ing like sir
ens go
ne ber

serk stuck for go
od inside
bodies bodies
turning col
d in hospital bed
room bed
s stiff in hos
pital mor
gue refri
gerators cubes of coff
ins plunk
ing down in
to the squ
are lat
rines of
grave
s
ca
plumk

what's left of thyr
sis and dorin
da tending flock
s of marvel
louos spect
ral sheep of
clouds in the e
lysian void up a
bove

angels

after a half third quarter
slept night near
dawn bent
over a notebook of yellow
paper quill in
hand scratching the surface from
time to time sometimes
desperately the damn itch not
going away scratching out
the accursed itchy
words with the maddeningly soft
tip of the quill till they bled their black
ink blood a treatise on
the baseness of man/great
ness of god rodrigo
martínez not knowing why not
knowing? yes knowing real
well heretofore unheard
inner voice calling calling
urgently get out get out you
fool fully
dressed as he'd laid
down jumped out of
bed stumbled out
of the cramped shabby
hut leaving the flimsy

door open hang
ing on one hinge showing for the whole
world to see the cramped shabby cluttered
inside a model of his own cramped shabby
cluttered mind saw in the luminous summer
morning on the verdant green
slope of the mountain on the other
side of the deep verdant
green valley big light
shapes moving aimless
ly lazily like cows
grazing cows? cows
from where in this
wilderness? from the
memory of the life left
behind? squinting his myopic
eyes didn't help the glasses
left on the table on top of the
notebook of yellow paper covered with
the black scabs of
words next to the black rotten
tooth stump of the burnt
out candle wouldn't
help either meant for
reading/writing the miserable
myopic/hyperopic practically
blind as a bat god's
creature hermit

crab his heart suddenly
pounding like crazy could
they be really? I mean could
they? after all these
years of waiting a proof? no
no yes yes yesss
spins around on one
foot runs like a madman is
one into the hut fumbles with his trembling
hand on the shelf for the
brass telescope bought brought
along for this exact
purpose can't find it where could it
be? it was here somewhere is here got
it spins around
again runs stumbles
on the doorstep loses one of
his loose worn silver buckled hidalgo
shoes stops pants pulls
out ever smaller
cylinders out of the bigger
ones no end to them puts
the end to his pale faded blue
ink trembling
eye expects to be
blinded by a blinding smiling
sapphire of an eye on the other
side immediately nearly falls

over backwards his heart
sinks drops to the very
bottom of the bottom
less pit there
staring back at him is a
huge round cosmic
boulder cold bare reddish
gray frightening like a full
moon seen through the
telescope in an empty night
sky such immense loneliness saw
it once who could stand it? couldn't
bear seeing it
again a hoped for angel's
eye

leipzig july 28

1 anna magda
lena wife 9 child
ren (catha
rina dorothe
a wilhelm friede
mann carl phil
ipp emanu
el gottfried hein
rich elisabeth ju
liana frideric
a johann christ
of friedrich jo
hann christ
ian johann
a carolina regi
na susanna) 1
share in
ursula erbs
tolln min
e 231 thal
ers in cash 25 in
medals 36 in pet
ty cash 65 in
debts 251 in sil
ver and oth
er valuables (can

dle sticks cup
s coffee tea
pot sug
ar bowl knive
s forks sp
oons sil
ver dagger gold
ring mo
re) 371 in in
struments (veneer
ed clavecin to st
ay in the fam
ily 4 mo
re laut
en werck lau
ten werck basset
gen spinett
gen 3 vio
lins 3 vio
las vio
la da gam
ba 2 vio
loncellos lu
te) 9 in pew
ter 7 cop
per brass 32 in
clothing (0 in 11
linen shirt

s) 29 in house
furnishings (6 tab
les dress
er chest ward
robe 18 chair
s writ
ing desk with
drawers 7
beds) 38 in theolo
gical book
s (caloviu
s luther müller tau
ler scheubler jo
sephus pfeiff
er stenger ram
bach more) for 11
22 grand
total less 1
52 owe
d but what a
bout the 10 fin
gers that pluck
ed grape
s of not
es from the vine
s of strings the 2 flee
t feet fleet
er than man

y any 10 fin
gers fly
ing over the foo
t pedals the w
hole man bent o
ver the table qu
ill in hand cha
sing dead s
lence off bl
ank sheets of pap
er as the bl
ack windy lei
pzig nigh
t knocked stub
bornly on the wind
ow pane with th
e sound of the b
ranches of the leaf
less tree out
side?

was
buried july 31 17
50 in johann
iskirche ce
metery for
gotten lost
found identi

fied by clay
molded over the
skull from 1
of 3 oak coff
ins re
buried in the johann
iskirche it
self in 1894 once
more in the thomas
kirche in 194
9 it was in st
thomas church on 5th
avenue I hear
d bigg e
power make peal
s of thunder mar
ch like con
scripts in a boot
camp to his mu
sic in
1963

on kicking the bucket

make sur
e you'v
e lost you
r family friend
s they
've lost
you you
they all go
ne no lov
e hard feeling
s left go
ne a blind
spot on the reti
na find a
room a per
fect cub
e emp
ty no door
s windows blind
ing bright white
walls crack
s in them li
ke gian
t crouch
ing spi
ders corners bla

ck smell
y like sweat
y arm
pits crotches a
n aid remind
er why
you're the
re a strong brand
new shiny eye
hook in the mid
dle of the cei
ling the ve
ry center a thick
soft gen
tle rope in
it noose on
the end the
knot loos
e sliding a
bucket plas
tic blue gr
een re
d zinc no
matter wha
t strong di
rectly under
neath it top
down wear

a comfort
able sui
t doub
le breast
ed prefer
ably more chest
room with
deep pock
s black navy
blue navy
blue preferred l
ess melodra
matic st
and on the buck
et pull
the noose o
ver you
r head a
round you
r neck ma
ke sure it
fits tight
en it feel
its soft
ness kind
ness feel
good stick both
hands in your pock

ets thrust
real deep hold on
to the lin
ing squee
ze squee
ze hard har
d hard
er don't
take a deep
breath ex
hale things will
speed up b
e easie
r close
your eyes jump
up kick
the bucket hear
it fly wai
t for what
's to co
me dark
ness don
't fig
ht don
't fig
ht ac
cept it keep
your hand

s in your po
ckets keep th
em closed squee
ze hard hard
hard
er hold on
to the lining in
no case ta
ke them ou
t try grab
bing the noos
e rope en
dure wait you
have no
choice for re
lief to
come it
will it
will in
the end it
will

on kicking the bucket once more

not et
ets more
than one a whole
bunch of
them ten
twleve two
dozen mo
re stood in
a circle in
a big emp
ty room hos
pital op
timally a
view of ward
s with end
less rows of wh
ite iron
beds corr
idors with mir
ror floors with
out end you
in the center look a
round see the cir
cle of buck
ets new zinc pre
ferred obli

gatory run up
to one of them sw
ing you
r leg wa
y back aim hit
the damne
d thin
g with a
ll you
r for
ce let i
t fly make a
noise so
und like a g
oose screa
ching that
's why you
want zin
c roll on
clatt
tter com
plain go for
the next
one do the
same wham ba
m ban
g it goes
flying roll

ling clatt

ttering ano

ther goos

e kicked in

the ass the rack

et from th

e firs

t one hasn

't died do

wn yet then th

e nex

t one one a

fter the other a

ll a

deaf

ening racket joy

of metal be

ing liv

ing out

side throu

gh the tall wi

de window

s a peace

ful gr

een eve

ning wit

h a red sun

set all a

round

on kicking the bucket in a different way

gent
ly let the bl
ood
red hand of
the sun
set on
the horizon sl
ip out of
your own f
eel its co
lor sha
pe smooth
ness gr
ow small
er small
er go
ne dit
to for the whi
te enamele
d one of the hos
pital be
d its lon
g cold pia
nist's fin
gers pr
ess you

r eye
sight ch
eek to the gr
een ghost
cheek of
the tree out
side then sl
owly sl
owly sl
ip out f
eet firs
t from bet
ween the
sheets a
long the steep
ly in
clined mat
tress in
to the wai
ting sp
ace be
low

just t
he warm
th left don'
t worr
y he's step

ped out for
a second will
be back
soo
n

brokenhaiku1
flower

such th

at it d

oesn't f

it into it

s color as i

nto a tigh

t dress

brokenhaiku2
moonlight

a
ncient whi
te eleph
ant moo
n wrink
led the lim
p trunk of it
s light dr
ags on th
e groun
d

brokenhaiku3
mountain brook

cl
ear you
whisp
er you
ex
ist

supreme gardener

be
hold his str
ong trans
parent hand pu
ll strug
gling lit
tle plan
ts out of the
ground dres
s them still st
ruggling in
to the cloth
es of shape
s colors gent
ly tug o
n wisp
s of leaves o
n the tip
s of branches
spread them in
to big g
reen plume
s make soil turn
over la
zily in it
s bed get read

y to get
up wa
ter in broo
ks sing in
a clear chan
ticleer child
's voi
ce whi
te cloud
s in the bl
ue sky fluf
f up look to
see where his st
eady non
existent fing
er points for
them to
go to

mountain

soil sto
ne dead
matter feel
ing the nee
d abi
lity to ri
se to
wer a
bove its nei
ghbors its
elf ris
ing form
ming o
n the fl
y slop
e heigh
t peak br
eathtak
ing vie
w of dul
l flat l
and be
low

cloud

soul of wa
ter you app
ear fr
om now
here in th
e clear s
ky and mo
ve in the di
rection on
ly you k
now in
different t
o una
ware of cas
ting a shad
ow on
us be
low

raindrop

from the cheek
no from hi
gh up from a
bove you b
ring the clear
ness of s
kies dis
tances of f
ar off
horizons cur
vatures of sof
t hills pic
ked up o
n the way d
own to de
posit them o
n our fac
es cheek
s take up r
oom tear
s want to occu
py

water

substance of z

eros clear dr

eam of opaque

matter star

t of tear

ful depart

ures end

of joy

ful arriv

als tan

gible visib

le time all cr

eatures cr

ave to be

you you

are and are

not

fish

next to no
far far a
way from t
he lake tree
s mountain
s s
ky big be
fore pit
ifully sm
all now f
its in the h
and emp
ty in
side a jagg
ed gash dow
n the death
ly white bell
y a flab
by lip
less mo
uth in a dr
owned man
's face

not the flow
er of wate
r a shrink

wrapped gift
wrapped wo
und

bird

tiny hand
full of co
lor feather
s flesh fresh
wound on a
branch throb
bing with s
ounds sing
ing prais
es to a blank
wall

stone

golden sun
sets of e
gypt its slan
ted o
cher rays pur
ple dusks vi
olets of par
is streets end
less gray po
lar arc
tic days ni
ghts the
ir calm
ing soft
light a red
rose lav
ender lil
ac bush pu
re white li
ly un
fading un
wilting strong
petalled e
ternal a s
tone is th
e flow
er of ti
me

flower

worn shab
by pet
als inde
terminable co
lor thin e
maciated s
tem face not
a cinderel
la of plant
s a poor
orphan gi
rl taking c
are of spoil
ed people
's dream
s

grass

the earth st
raining to th
e ut
most try
ing to b
e eart
h swoll
en red the
grass ug
ly like bulg
ing bright g
reen e
yes

old cemetery

a
boat too
heavy over
loaded up
to the gun
wales in gra
ss it
sails thr
ough the roug
h sea of gre
en it spla
shes spill
s in
side near
ly fill
s it the
dead stand
chest dee
p grin
ning ear to
ear they will
not can
not drown

your dead

your dea
d father mo
ther friend who
ever have
not abandon
ed you are not
gone they'
re there wait
ing pati
ent will
ing read
y to d
o what they c
an scenes from
your past like
squares on the si
des of a tria
ngle in a text
book of geo
metry balance them
selves on the
ir outlines a g
lass of lemon
ade pressed to
your lips as y
ou lay on t

he sofa sick wi
th high fev
er a gam
e of chess play
ed at a picnic in
the count
ry in tall gr
ass a hand w
aving fro
m a dark door
way for th
e last t
ime

rose1

a love
letter crump
led up in a cramp
ed hand a
bloody little
rag stink
ing of the
gasoline flow
ers run o
n a tempo
rary name th
at ultimate
ly turns to
fell like a
ll that ris
es in the e
nd it f
all
s

rose2

christ of pl
ants sacrifi
ced in the co
zy golgotha
s of gard
ens cru
cified on its
own shap
e a crow
n of its
thorns on it
s head all wound
s giving off per
fume in
stead of drip
ping blood

rose3

filling in s
quares color r
ed odor a
greeable shape ye
s compo
nent parts pe
tals stamens pist
il leaves stem
s branches r
oots a decon
structed ro
se is a sta
tistic not a tra
gedy

sillysong1

the t
rain start
ed an
d the worl
d swayed l
ike tea
rs y
ou wave
d your ro
secolor
ed scar
f leaning ou
t the wind
ow the co
lor of
my lips was l
ike a to
rn faded s
carf h
eld in m
y teet
h

sillysong2

in lil
ac du
sk amo
ng lil
ac bush
es i sear
ched f
or you
r lil
ac eyes m
y hear
t twing
ed wi
th fear i w
ouldn't fi
nd them t
o the e
ar pierc
ing calls o
f the night
ingale

sillysong3

to the e

dge of t

own you

saw me o

ff t

o the e

dge of t

own you

r han

d was l

ike a wh

ite dov

e grow

ing sm

aller and sm

aller a

s it tri

ed to fo

low me wh

ile i wal

ked on

dreamdream1

i'm in an or
chard or
something walk a
mong trees a lit
tle boy sudd
enly springs up b
efore me sm
all half m
y size eyes the
whole face smil
ing look
ing up at me i
realize it
's my fath
er who die
ed years ago no
thing strange ab
out it stran
ge that he's a
child he wan
ts to play gr
abs my hand pulls
me along co
me let's p
lay laughs i le
t myself be pu

lled but feel re
luctant the
re's some
thing wrong a
bout it he's m
y father af
ter all he
keeps on pull
ing me ur
ging come c
ome run sud
denly again he let
s go of my
hand and run
s real fast laugh
ing i'm con
cerned he runs too
fast may fa
ll down h
urt himself i ye
ll slow
down slow
down you'
ll hurt you
r self he does
n't listen run
s laugh
s there's a wood

en shack up a
head sm
all more lik
e an out
house than a
shack he runs a
round it now real
ly fast he's b
ound to hurt him
self sto
p dad sto
p i yell the
back of my n
eck num
b stop he
doesn't listen dis
appears be
hind the ed
ge of the st
ructure i
run like ma
d after him ro
und the corner th
ere in th
e tall grass he
lies face
down some
thing dark shi

ny wet can be
seen on the grou
nd next to
his hea
d i bend d
own look y
es it's bl
ood the
re's a big ro
ck in the grass nex
t to his head he
fell and cra
cked his head o
pen on it i s
ee his sku
ll is spl
it open some
thing white l
ike magg
ots stirs in
side it it's h
is brains they
're still ali
ve that'
s why they mo
ve but he's
gone for sure can't re
cover from an inju

ry like that i stra
ighten up wal
k away the
re's no poin
t in my stay
ing i can't help
him the sc
ene around
me is different
now grassy like a sa
vannah tall t
rees with slend
er trunks li
ke palms grow he
re and there bend
ing graceful
ly i look with curi
osity no they
're not palm tr
ees they're hu
ge dande
lions with gian
t white puf
fs on top a gus
t of wind come
s blowing some
seeds detach th
emselves float o

ff like white pa
rachutes into the
sky it's full of th
em and of whi
te clouds the
y look the
same you can
't tell the two a
part they're so
beautiful in
the blue sky life
's so beauti
ful i walk
on

dreamdream2

it's late eve
ning dusk not
early dawn for
sure it's cer
tain it'll get dark
er there's a thin r
ed and gold
streak way on
the horizon as wh
en the sun sets so
it must be dus
k i'm in a field v
ast flat plow
ed digging with a sp
ade in the grou
nd there's a wo
man next to
me on my lef
t it's my mo
ther whom i've ne
ver seen she die
d before i was born i
mean giving b
irth to me i turn to
look at her she's
dumpy old dressed like a

peasant woman in a lon
g skirt and a ker
chief she's ben
ding down sud
denly she straight
ens up and loo
ks at me her face is
young young
for my mother'
s friendl
y i'm pleased i
have a mother t
oo finally and so young
looking she
smiles her teet
h are white like t
he kerchief on h
er head look heal
thy i smile back we
go back to diggin
g my spade hi
ts something h
ard i bend down p
ick it up it l
ooks like a pota
to round and gra
y i straight
en up and look at

the thing turn
it around in my fin
gers it's cake
d with dirt with ho
les in it look
s strange for a po
tato my mother takes
it from me and clean
s it off it's a tiny hu
man skull the siz
e of a pota
to she says we ha
ve to dig the
se up they
're all over it's
a cemetery we
have to clea
r it for new gr
aves she toss
es it over her should
er and goes back
to digging i do th
e same we keep on dig
ging find sk
ulls and toss them be
hind us it goes on
like that the light
gets dark

er in the end yo
u can't s
ee anything then th
e scene chang
es i'm in a big
peasant style kit
chen next t
o a stove my mo
ther's on my left the
re's a huge pot on
top of the stov
e steam's co
ming out of it she's cook
in something it must
be potatoes there's
that unpleasant sm
ell of boiled pota
toes in the air then
she's pushing some
thing hot and round in
to my mouth i don'
t want it it's too
hot and i don't like b
oiled potatoes but
it feels differ
ent than a po
tato it's hard li
ke an egg re

minds me of so
me thing i lean b
ack and look
at it it's one of
the skulls we
were digging up it'
s crazy why is
she feeding i
t to me? she pushes
it back against m
y lips i keep them
shut keep leaning
back she per
sist tells me to o
pen my m
outh take a bi
te it's goo
d i won't do it th
ough get ang
ry try to push
her hand away sh
e resists keeps
on pressing the th
ing against my lips t
eeth a little more and
she'll succeed i grab
her hand pull i
t away angri

ly scream st
o stop sto
p what mo
ther would fee
d her son boil
ed skulls?

dreamdream3

i walk along the
beach it's l
ike in the fin
al scene of fellini
's la dolce vi
ta flat emp
ty the sea on the
left rough a
low gray sky a
bove strong wind
blows off the wa
ter the sea is f
ull of white
caps my hair b
lows gets i
n my eyes i
squint sud
denly a black dot ap
pears in the dis
tance a hu
man fig
ure on the ed
ge of the water it
grows as i near
it seems slen
der tall with lon

g blond h
air a young wo
man in a long whi
te dress like a ro
man toga? yes that
's what it is i s
ee as i come near
her she stands with
her back to
me doesn't s
ee me i come up
to her stop t
urn her a
round her
face is like a draw
ing done with a sh
arp pencil on crys
tal clerar wa
ter barely dis
tinguish
able but per
fect beau
tiful she smi
les her hair stream
s in the wind en
velops me we're
joined by it i
try to kiss her can'

t find her lips she lau
ghs it doesn'
t matter there
'll be time f
or that we
move on w
ith our arm
s around each o
ther she's th
e one i've b
een looki
ng for all my
life now i've foun
d her i never th
ought i would now
we're one the
wind keeps on blow
ing gets stron
ger the sea
rougher the spray
envelops us we g
et all wet cling to
each other laug
h it's fun but sud
denly there
s' water all a
round us it's as
if we're on a boat

it heaves under
us tilts this
way and that goes
up and down waves
spill over us i'm a
fraid they'll w
ash us away separa
te us we cling to
each other i grab onto
something stea
dy like a rail
ing with one
hand clutch her to
me with the o
ther the wa
ter keeps on co
ming i hold on to
her with all my
might but the
sea's strong strong
er than me th
en a huge wave spill
s over us there
's water all a
round we've bee
n washed away in
to the sea sepa
rated she's go

ne i'm des
perate try to stay a
float but search
for her with my
eyes don't see
her it can't
be that i've lost
he i've just found
her i open my mou
th to scream to
call for her grow
cold i don't kn
ow her name how
can i call for
her find her if i
don't know her
name?

tiger1

feral ro
se of f
lesh fur t
eeth you b
loom in t
he garden
s of our dream
s scream
s of wild an
imals soul
s in des
pair stream
ing in fr
om a
far

tiger2

a qui
et afternoon i
n the offic
e john do
e shut the doo
r dozed off d
reamt a gre
at big tige
r came alon
g squirt
ed pee
d on his sh
irt heart th
en qui
etly slink
ed a
way

tiger3

so sa
d old fad
ed stripes fray
ed whisk
ers fur lim
p tail slack
jaw head h
ung down l
ow read
y for an art
ist's ey
e hand t
o mov
e you fr
om the c
age in
to a fram
e be
hind gla
ss on
to a shee
t of rice pa
per

cityscape1

flat black tar
red roofs n
ext to e
ach oth
er as far a
s the e
ye can s
ee in al
l direct
ions crumb
ling brick chim
neys lik
e al
l that's left
of dwell
ings on so
me of the
m clus
ters of thin decap
itated cros
ses of tv ant
ennas her
e and th
ere a bl
ock or s
o a

way on on
e of the r
oofs a huge p
ale worm sqirm
ing thrash
ing about i
n agony sud
denly it brea
ks up ri
ses no no
t a wor
m a coupl
e making lo
no fuck
ing

beneath a
sky
blue sky

cityscape2

seen from a g
reat height he
aps of blood
smeared bric
ks stretching
all the way t
o the horizon
flattened strip
s of chrome
plated rivers
here and ther
e rusty overt
urned truss b
ridges a mos
quito sized p
lane has pun
ctured throug
h the rubber
membrane of
clouds and is
frantically try
ing to find its
way back up

cityscape3

flat sea of b
ricks in t
he distan
ce sharp spir
es stick
ing up in pl
aces like arm
s of people dro
wning cal
ing for hel
p cit
y halls? church
es? clos
e up on the w
all of an ab
andoned ware
house a gra
ffiti in beaut
fully draw
n big wh
ite letters rim
med in black pro
claims god s
ucks

seascape1

a shiny d
ark gray h
orizontal pl
ane cut o
ff by a dul
l light vert
ical one i
n the dist
ance a stro
ng smell of fr
esh oil p
aint in t
he air the s
ound of hea
vy workers
' footst
eps loud
voices door
s wind
ows bang
ing in the st
rong draf
t

seascape2

the sun lo
st in the p
ure blue s
ky the s
ea getting
up and fall
ing dow
n hea
vily out o
f breat
h ear
piercing c
ries of p
pain lik
e calls of sea
gulls

seascape3

dunes drift
wood rust
y tin cans a
ll sort of gar
bage steal
ing up to t
he ed
ge of wa
ter a tin
y hu
man figu
re walk
ing alon
g its sur
face near
ing the hor
izon

dawn

the white of b
roken tib
ias be
ing stack
ed up in on
e spot o
n the horiz
on in th
e east it gr
ows spi
lls over west
ward the squ
ealing of bi
rds at
tests to the i
ntensity o
f the pai
n

sunsets

not macabr
e blood
y rituals ce
line witness
ed in africa e
vening af
ter even
ing worse
than th
at dai
ly spon
taneous a
bortions mis
carriage
s of day
s

dusk

gone the res
t of bri
ghtness ho
pe on the ho
rizon the sp
ace fill
ed with ro
ugh con
crete wa
lls wi
de a
part on
ly f
or cheek
s to squee
ze them
selves in to
tight
ly press a
gainst

god is

an a
theist a reg
ular down
to earth meat a
nd potat
os guy too
busy for sil
ly sentiment
al theories likes
to roll up his sl
eeves get dow
n to the nit
ty gritty mole
cules elec
trons prot
ons neut
rons quar
ks str
ings that vib
rate sound
like ang
ry kill
er bees

the world is not

an effect it
has no ca
use could n
ot have o
ne wh
ere w
ould it t
he caus
e h
ave bee
n cre
ating i
t? if i
t was i
nside t
he worl
d it w
as part o
f it it
just chan
ged it
self t
hat's a
ll
a cau
se ca

nnot b

e its o

wn eff

ect

chores

was
born breath
ed in op
end my eyes c
ried ate gr
ew wal
ked spo
ke wen
t to schoo
l grad
uated got
a job w
ife had
kids buil
t a hous
e ti
red re
tired all
done sh
it n
o for
got still hav
e to die

blackblacknight1

stink
ing skin
ny black o
ld she goa
t of the nigh
t bleats baa
a baaa b
aaa as t
hey lead h
er to t
he cemeter
y to mil
k her fee
d her bl
ack mi
lk to t
he dea
d

reflect
ions of drop
pings i
n the star
less sk
y

blackblacknight2

dad what a
re th
ose soun
ds you h
ear com
ing fro
m the gr
aveyard i
n the mid
dle of t
he night? i
t's th
e de
ad try
ing to s
peak w
ith their mo
uths stuff
ffed w
ith the b
lack pota
to o
f dea
th

blackblacknight3

they grab t
hem god kn
ows wh
o or wh
y wh
en the
y least ex
pect it hol
d t
hem tigh
t cov
er the
ir mouth
s w
ith the
ir hand
s to kee
p them q
uiet lead th
em tout de
suite to t
he ceme
tery ti
e th
em up r
eal t

ight in
side with s
trong stro
ng twi
ne lay t
hem dow
n on the
ir back
s in th
ese nea
t squa
re holes i
n the g
round to fa
ce th
e star
less sk
y to sc
are them an
d stuff the
ir mouth
s with th
e nigh
t t
ied in
to a bi
g ti
ght wad s

o th
at th
ey can'
t screa
m

death/blue car

she lead m
e down a d
ark corrid
or to a sm
all room it
s walls fac
ed with ch
eap br
own pan
eling you'
ll die here s
he said a
nd walk
ed out the d
oor closing i
t be
hind h
er a mili
tary iro
n bed cov
ered with a b
lanket wi
th a pill
ow on it st
ood in on
e corner i r

emained stand

ing for a f

ew second

s looking a

round an

d then decid

ed to lie d

own ther

e was no p

oint in pro

crastinat

ing af

ter anoth

er few sec

onds i rais

ed myself how

ever and cra

ning my nec

k looked ou

t the wind

ow i

t was a w

et gloom

y day out

side ne

xt to a delap

idated wood

en she

d once re
d now mor
e like gr
ay stood a
n old rus
ty bl
ue car sunk
en to the fl
oorboard in
to the gr
ound

die young

die young seven
teen six
teen young
er what
ever go to
bed with
your six
ty year old ugh
ly science teach
er feel guilt
y dis
gusted thr
ow up at the
memory of he
r moans squirm
ing crotch chok
e on your vom
it die
young fifteen four
teen young
er what
ever blow you
r brains out be
hind the tall ro
se bush just af
ter kissing for th

e firs
t t
ime the beau
tiful fifteen four
teen whate
ver year
old cou
sin of your b
est friend the t
aste of the ed
ge of her flutt
ering butter
fly soul fresh
on your lip
s d
ie young nine
ten young
er hold
ing your brea
th in amaze
ment seeing
for the first
time a flow
er come out
of the g
round watch
ing it bloom
blush die

young five six
months old young
er wrench your
self from you
r fat
her's strong h
ands while he b
ounces you o
n his knee p
laying hop
along cas
sidy plung
e head fir
st on the nia
gara of your gig
gles break
your neck on
the floo
r die you
ng be
fore you'v
e noticed that
the facult
ies of your bod
y and mind h
ave been van
ishing on
e by o

ne like neigh
bors in the build
ing you live i
n moving o
ut leaving
you al
l a
lone before
your skin look
s just like you
r father's in old
age yellow with dark
spots like flies in
ointment before
strange ug
ly bumps ap
pear on your hand
s from now
here that hav
e no meaning or pur
pose before g
aps appear in you
r mouth where tee
th once grew l
ike big vac
ant lots be
fore you notic
e you're get

ting small
er and small
er like an i
ce cube in war
m water and f
ear you'll disa
ppear altoge
ther be
fore you
r nose and ears k
eep getting big
ger and big
ger and you
fear they'll ne
ver stop grow
ing be
fore drop
s of clear liqu
id start appear
ing on the end of
your nose like tear
s even though no
ses don't cry be
fore your no
se keeps trying to
join your chi
n and the oth
er way aroun

d and both are su
cceeding before you
realize one day peop
le aren't talk
ing softer bu
t that it's ge
tting hard for
you to hear before
blinking does
n't make you see
better before
you notice you
look like a capital
letter s when you
're standing up stra
ight before you loo
k like a question
mark whether or
not you're ask
ing something or sit
ting down bef
ore you
notice there a
re fewer and few
er people lef
t you know be
fore you learn th
e names of more a

nd more new disease

s before the wor

d sick takes on a

totally ne

w meaning and you real

ize this one is fin

ally right before t

hey for

get you have a l

ast name and c

all you on

ly by you

r first befo

re they start stick

ing needles in

to you for no reas

on unless it be

to find the

most pain

ful spot before

they've discover

ed there's a big

demand for your

blood and they

try to fill

it before

they start dres

sing you in wi

res and tubes and god
knows what to ma
ke you look fun
ny weird before
they st
art teaching you to
stretch out and
lie still and cl
ose your e
yes and turn
white and not
breath
e before you
die

little fugue

from outer inn
er space regard
less the gl
obe look
s like a b
ig round hea
d crawling w
ith frantic sh
apes live h
air? ant
s? an ant
heap some
one stepped in
to? no peo
ple all of hum
anity every on
e runs runs ru
ns after from it
's a chase f
light latin fu
ga from fu
gare fugere fr
om the mo
ment you're bor
n to the ins
tant you d

ie after wha
t you can't rea
ch from that thump
thump of feet wh
eez wheez of
breath clat c
lat of bo
es whose bo
nes? you kno
w whose just be
hind you john
runs jogs in the mor
ning to stay in
shape be up to t
he demand
s of his job life jan
e at night to loo
k good catch
john or some
one else a
bebe runs bare
foot for g
old in rome gret
e in high
tech shoes f
or a big car b
igger bucks in cen
tral park 45

000 run lim
p with her f
or fame p
ain kamerad
erie the hec
k of it ba
rak runs fo
r president to s
ave the count
ry from the other
s hillary joh
n mitt the o
thers ditto the s
ame bernie r
uns after his
friends the
ir your mo
ney rich
es a coupl
e more yacht
s florida ho
mes little bob
by runs to mo
mmy to hu
g her fee
l safe mo
mmy runs a
round like cra

zy from mor
ning till nigh
t to from sch
ool pian
o ballet sci
ence chin
ese lesson so
ccer hockey gym
nastics pra
ctice her yo
ga class a ty
pical piano ball
et science ch
inese less
on socce
r hockey gym
nastics yoga p
racticing mo
m daddy ru
ns for the school
board to be bor
ed on it like a
ll the other
s then the ci
ty council st
ate assemb
ly congr
ess why st

op there? bren
da runs away fr
om home t
o shack u
p with her
gas pump a
ttendant boyf
riend brad to
ny runs the gas
station to mak
e a living a
nd make li
fe hard for
brad marc
ia despit
e all appearanc
es runs the s
how most prob
ably because o
f her first
name she wears p
ants in the fam
ily too in ad
dition to under
pants of cour
se rob
ert rabbit
runs scare

d all his li
fe definit
ely because of h
is last brian run
s for his lif
e because he he
ars a shell com
ing sally run
s to the bat
hroom be
cause she h
as an infect
ion and a sm
all bladd
er to boo
t stuart runs t
o catch the bu
s so as not t
o be late in
the office on
ce again julia
runs up the
steps in hol
lywood to fin
ally get her os
car gaby dit
to in stock
holm fo

r his no
bel prize dip
loma med
al check the
y stretc
h out their h
ands c
lose th
eir fingers b
ut that's no
t it e
nough the chase f
light goes on t
hen one day w
hen you leas
t expect it pres
to she's righ
t there be
hind be
fore them y
ou us all pres
sed up tigh
t snap z
ap she's got
us we're g
one or as uk
rainians say xoch
kr

ut' xo
ch vert' znaj
desh sob
i u cherepoch
ku smer
t' or you
can tw
ist and you c
an turn but i
n the end you
'll wind u
p in a
n urn

pretty long f
or a littl
e fugu
e hu
h
?

ABOUT THE AUTHOR

Yuriy Tarnawsky has authored twenty collections of poetry, eight books of fiction, seven plays, a biography, and numerous articles and translations. An engineer and linguist by training, he has worked as computer scientist specializing in Natural Language Processing and Artificial Intelligence at IBM Corporation as well as Professor of Ukrainian Literature and Culture at Columbia University in New York City. He was born in Ukraine and raised in the West. He writes in Ukrainian and English and resides in the vicinity of New York City. His English-language books include the novel, *Three Blondes and Death*; a collection of stories, *Short Tails*; three collections of mininovels, *The Placebo Effect Trilogy*; and the play, *Not Medea*.